For Julien, Baptiste, Pierre and Dora

With thanks to Isabelle Cahn, Céline Julhiet-Charvet, Clémence Berg, Anne de Margerie and Jean.

Published by Peter Bedrick Books
2112 Broadway, New York, NY 10023

All art is from work of Cézanne except the print on page 50.
Layout and design: Thomas Gravemaker, X-Act

ISBN 0-87226-476-9
CIP Data is available from the Library of Congress

Printed in Mexico
5 4 3 2 1 96 97 98 99
First American Edition

Cézanne from A to Z

Marie Sellier

Translated from the French by
Claudia Zoe Bedrick

PETER BEDRICK BOOKS
NEW YORK

Contents

Accent du Midi
The Flavor of the South

Baignades
Bathers

Hortense
Cézanne's Wife

Impressionnistes
Impressionists

Jas du Bouffan
His Father's House

Kilos de pommes
Pounds of Apples

Lignes droites
Straight Lines

Rupture
Break

Sainte-Victoire
A Mountain in Aix

Touches
Daubs

hUé
Jeered

Va-et-vient
Vacillation

Contrarié
Opposed

Décor
Decoration

États d'âme
Moods

Flamme
Enthusiasm

Galerie de portraits
Portrait Gallery

Mise en scène
Setting

Nus au bain
Nude Bathers

Ocre
Ochre

Plein air
Out-of-doors

Quatre-vingt-quinze
'95

Wagner

aiX

Yeux
Eyes

oseZ
Let Us Dare

Crédits photos
Acknowledgments

Accent du Midi

The Flavor of the South

Louis-Auguste, Paul Cézanne's father.

Our story begins in Aix-en-Provence, on January 19, 1839, with the birth of the boy who will become the famous painter, Paul Cézanne. His father, Louis-Auguste Cézanne, has a profitable business selling bowler hats, top-hats, and military caps. When Paul is still a boy, his father buys Aix's only bank, thus becoming a small-town banker. This is quite an achievement for a

In the nineteenth century, everyone wore hats.

man who is the son of Italian immigrants and never went to school. Louis-Auguste's intention is for Paul to follow in his footsteps. To begin with, Paul does not disappoint his father. He is a good student and wins numerous prizes, not in painting, but in some of his favorite subjects, such as Latin and Greek.

Far from Paris, Aix is at this time a small, peaceful town, almost a village, surrounded by hills, vineyards, and cypresses.

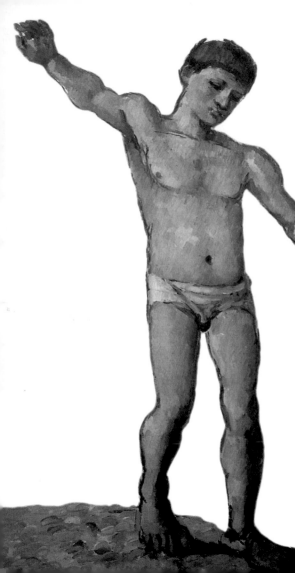

Baignades

Bathers

One day, when he is in the courtyard of his high-school, the Collège Bourbon, the thirteen year old Paul defends a small boy who is being teased by some of his classmates. This boy is only a year younger than Paul, but he is unusually thin and very near-sighted. His name is Émile Zola. Émile and Paul quickly become inseparable. Their greatest happiness is to set off in the early morning, along with their friend Baptistin, to wander the Aix countryside. Through their rambles, they come to know every stream and watering hole, even those concealed in shadowy ravines. What they love

Detail from *Bather with Arms at His Sides.*

Detail of an illustrated letter from
Cézanne to Zola.

most is to splash around in
the water after a long walk,
or to have a water-fight
before drying off in the hot
sun. For them, the height of
perfection is to end the day
under a tree reading aloud
the poems which they love,
and discussing projects and
their future, in which
everything seems possible
and where, without a doubt,
fame awaits them.

Paul, the future painter, and Émile, the future writer,
share a passion for water.

Contrarié

Opposed

In 1857, when he enrolls in Aix's free drawing academy, Paul is 18 years old. Although his work at the academy does not keep him from passing his baccalauréat exams with success the following year, he nevertheless has come to realize that his way lies in painting. He confides his desire to become a painter to Zola, who has left Aix to live in Paris with his mother. Paul would like to join his friend in Paris, but his father has other plans for him. Louis-Auguste has already decided that his only

Paul draws with passion, using objects as well as live models as his subjects.

son will study law. Therefore, Paul's future is not open to discussion. It has been settled. Paul defers to his gruff, authoritarian father, whom, more than anything, he fears. He enrolls in the faculty of law, but continues to follow his painting course with the silent blessings of his mother.

Detail of a portrait that Paul does of his father in 1866.

Décor

Decoration

For Paul, the study of law turns out to be a nightmare. He does not wish to disappoint his father, but he becomes less and less able to pretend. Unable to do otherwise, he abandons his books for pencils and paintbrushes. The decoration of the Jas de Bouffan, the beautiful house near Aix which his father purchases in 1859, provides him with the opportunity to make his first large-scale attempts. Paul does not hesitate. He paints four panels representing the four seasons directly on to the wall of the salon. What is most surprising is that the severe Louis-Auguste does not oppose him. Now more than ever, Paul feels that he must go to Paris to paint seriously. In his father's presence, Paul is sullen and hostile. He stays out as much as he can, and when he is home, he refuses to talk. The situation quickly becomes unbearable. In the end, Paul's father gives in. At the end of April, 1861, Paul leaves for Paris.

In a burst of youthful irreverence, Paul signs his panels with the name of Ingres, a painter whom he does not admire at all. Does he mock Ingres or himself?

États d'âme

Moods

Paul is disappointed. The Paris to which he has come is not the city of his dreams. He finds life difficult, living alone as he does on barely sufficient means. Most disappointing of all is the fact that he and Zola are unable to re-establish the harmony of their youth. Émile is friendly and attentive, but he has his own life. He writes, has his own friends, and so is unable to devote himself fully to Cézanne. After only a brief period, Paul's only concern is to return to Aix. To help prolong Cézanne's stay in Paris, Zola asks him to paint his portrait. Paul agrees. In the end, he dislikes the painting and is deeply

In 1861, Paul paints this tormented self-portrait.

discouraged. In a fit of rage, Cézanne destroys the portrait with his palette knife. He feels that he is finished. He packs his suitcases and prepares to leave the capital of salons and fashionable cafes. He has failed. Therefore, he will return to Aix to work in his father's bank. The demon of painting, however, refuses to relinquish its hold on him. Just a few months later, he returns to Paris, with his paint-brushes and a passion to paint.

Quai de Bercy. Cézanne finds Paris quite gray compared to the warmth and sun of Provence.

Émile Zola

15

Flamme

Enthusiasm

Vénus, after Raphael. "The Louvre is a good book to consult," says Paul, who copies a number of masterpieces there.

Settled in Paris once again, Paul frequents the Swiss Studio, where he benefits from reasonably priced models. He goes there every day, morning and evening, to draw nudes and to study models of the human body. He also goes frequently to the Louvre to look at the works of the painters whom he admires, such as Eugène Delacroix and Nicolas Poussin. Upon returning to his studio, he constructs large compositions of fantastic scenes, in which vivid colors boldly confront each other. At this time, Cézanne also begins to paint

One of Cézanne's favorite models is Scipio, an African whose muscled body he finds to be a magnificent lesson in anatomy.

still-lifes of everyday objects which he finds in his surroundings. His father would like him to enter the school of Beaux-Arts, but Paul has too much contempt for official art to do so. He prefers to make friends with Camille Pissarro, Auguste Renoir, and Claude Monet, and to admire the free and powerful work of Édouard Manet, painters all of whom have had their works refused by the Salons.

Galerie de

Portrait Gallery

As early as 1863, Cézanne begins to divide his time between Paris and Aix, where he spends part of the year with his family. There, his uncle Dominique, his mother's brother, poses as his model. For Paul's benefit, his uncle dons many different disguises, all of which are dreamed-up by Paul. Uncle Dominique transforms himself into a monk, a lawyer or a craftsman. Leaving his paintbrush to the side, Cézanne works on faces with a knife, sculpting them out of a thick paste. Cézanne also begins to

1866, Uncle Dominique as a lawyer.

portraits

grapple with large-format paintings. He paints a portrait of his friend, Achille Emperaire, the Aixois painter, on a canvas that is slightly more than six-and-a-half feet high. What makes this portrait strange is the fact that Cézanne does not try to minimize Emperaire's physical deformity. Rather, the attitude and strongly determined contours of the figure, along with the vibrant and contrasting colors of his clothing, lead one to think more of a caricature than of a portrait.

Punning, Cézanne paints Achille Emperaire as a mocking emperor on his throne.

Hortense

Cézanne's wife

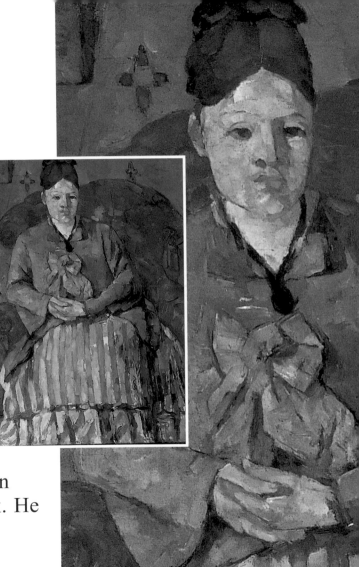

The moody Cézanne has always been intimidated by women. Nevertheless, in 1869, he succumbs to the charms of his nineteen year old model, Hortense Fiquet, with whom he falls in love. Without breathing a word to his father, he moves in with her. He is thirty years old. When the war of 1870 breaks out, he flees with Hortense to L'Estaque, a small village near Marseilles. He does not care in the least if he is considered a deserter. He has no interest in fighting. More than anything, he wants to continue his work. He

View from L'Estaque.

does so, painting the red roofs of the houses of L'Estaque, which overhang the blue waters of the Mediterranean. Two years later, in January 1872, Cézanne becomes a father. He names his son, Paul, after himself. It is not until 1886, however, that Paul and Hortense become husband and wife. With marriage, Cézanne's habits change hardly at all. Solitary he is and solitary he will remain.

At 33, Cézanne is still so afraid of his father that he keeps the birth of his son from him.

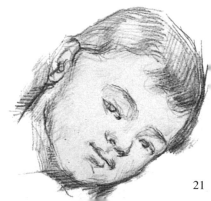

Hortense

21

Impressionistes

Impressionists

Through the efforts of Camille Pissarro, Cézanne is won-over to a small group of avant-garde painters. In the group are Renoir, Monet and Sisley. Their aspiration is to paint in a way that will bring them into closer contact with nature. Their aim is to paint their subject as they see and feel it. In Pontoise and then in Auvers-sur-Oise, where he lives for a time with them, Cézanne participates in their experiments. He paints outside, more rapidly than is

"The humble and colossal Pissarro," is how Cézanne refers to his painter friend.

At center, Cézanne, to the right, Pissarro, in the company of two other painters.

The Bridge at Maincy. A palette of greens and yellows renders the play of leaves and water.

his habit and more freely. Deeply moved by the play of light, he softens his palette. He discovers that color is able to define an object as effectively as line. In 1874, tired of the systematic refusal of his paintings by the official Salons, Paul, along with his friends, takes part in an independent exhibition. There the now-famous name "Impressionist" is launched, coined from a painting by Monet entitled, "Impression," in derision of the works exhibited by the avant-garde painters.

Jas de

His Father's House

Jas de Bouffan means "house of winds."

When he is in Aix, Paul lives at the Jas de Bouffan, his father's estate. The house, which was previously the residence of the governor of Provence, is surrounded by grand old trees. During the winter, Cézanne's beloved Mount Sainte-Victoire is reflected in the water of an elaborate basin ornamented with

Bouffan

stone dolphins and lions. At the Jas de Bouffan, far from the influences of other painters, Cézanne feels at peace and able to create. At times, in order to realize his vision, Cézanne has the agricultural workers of the area pose for him. Such workers, humble and anonymous, serve as models for his painting, *The Card Players*. To pursue his studies in painting, Cézanne requires a great deal of solitude. One wonders whether without his retreats to the Jas de Bouffan, Cézanne would have become as clearly distinct from his Impressionist friends as he did.

Kilos de Pommes

Pounds of Apples

Throughout his life, Cézanne paints apples, ordinary red, yellow and green apples such as one buys at the market. For Cézanne, this fruit is tied to a happy memory. Many years earlier, in thanks for standing up for him in the courtyard of the Collège Bourbon, Émile Zola had given

Cézanne a basket full of apples. Cézanne is content for people to think that he paints apples in homage to the great friendship of his youth. Yet, for him, the apple is really far more than that. It is his supreme model, far less intimidating than a female model. The apple, with its contours, lends itself to all compositions. It constitutes a marvelous subject of observation and study for a painter who never ceases to work on form, color and light.

"I wish to conquer Paris with an apple," says Paul.

Lignes droites

Straight Lines

In painting, Cézanne achieves the precision and rigor of the great builders. His paintings are always firmly constructed. He is similar to an architect or a mason. Straight lines—horizontal, vertical, and oblique—define his planes, joining them into triangles, squares, rectangles and other geometrical figures. It is not by chance that Cézanne paints so many houses. The edges of facades, as well as roofs, windows and doors permit him to

Cézanne does not wish to paint "fuzzy" paintings, such as those of the Impressionists.

delimit areas of color, to play with planes and to create variations of light. The rigor of construction is not all that is involved, however. Something else is necessary to render the air's purity or the heat of Provence's sun. Cezanne's paintings go beyond geometry to capture the elusive quality of light itself.

At the end of his life, Cézanne will say that everything in nature can be treated "through the cylinder, the sphere, the cone."

Cézanne is more at ease with objects than with people. His interest is in rendering the atmosphere of things.

Mise en

Setting

Cézanne is a master at the art of setting the scene. He arranges his still-lifes with the precision of a set-designer who organizes each detail of a production. No object appears by chance. Each has its specific role to play in the composition. Cézanne is careful and takes his time to choose what will best complement the apples, oranges and onions which he has decided to paint. Will it be this clay pitcher or that wicker basket? This

scène

tin kettle or that bottle of wine? This skull or that small plaster angel? He chooses according to his mood, preferring a white cloth with well-defined folds, a wrinkled napkin, colored fabric, patterned paper, or the bare surface of a wooden table. As he himself says: objects live, grow familiar, talk between themselves. To get a sense of the "dust of emotion" which surrounds them, one must pay close attention.

So that they will "keep their pose," Cézanne plunges his napkins into a plaster bath.

Nus au bain

Nude Bathers

In Cézanne's body of work, paintings and watercolors depicting bathers return like a refrain. There are no less than 140 such paintings. These figures arise from Cézanne's memory of going swimming with Émile and Baptistin in his youth. Around Cézanne's bathers, the countryside is calm and green. It seems as though it is summer, but it is not clear what the location is: the outskirts of Paris? Provence? It does not really matter. What is

1874, *Five Bathers.*

important are the nude figures, which are not copied by Cézanne, but arranged out of his imagination: from front to back, in a smaller or greater number, sitting or standing. The situations vary, as if Cézanne is seeking an ideal composition, as if he seeks, from canvas to canvas, to breathe life into his bathers, to give them soul.

Cézanne at the end of his life in front of his monumental *Bathers*, after years of experimenting with the simplification of forms.

Ocre

Ochre

Ochre, neither yellow, nor brown, nor red. The color of clay, of earth, of sand. Of all the colors used by Cézanne, it is the one most characteristic of him. It gives his greens and blues their specific quality, and its affect is to illuminate faces, skies, the fronts of buildings and the arid earth. It is the color of the rocks of the Bibémus quarry, that cascade of cubed rocks which Cézanne so loves to paint. It also is the color of the facade of the Château Noir,

Château Noir

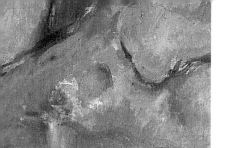

Bibémus quarry.

that great ramshackle house painted by Cézanne emerging from a screen of green. It is the color of Provence's sun, whose light suffuses his paintings.

The bodies of his bathers are ochre as well.

Plein air

Out-of-doors

"You see," confides Cézanne to Zola in 1866, "all the paintings done inside, in the studio, will never match those done outdoors." Along with his Impressionist friends, Cézanne develops the habit of going outside to paint his model, which is nature in its own setting. Well after his path has diverged from that of the Impressionists, he continues to paint outdoors in order to paint what he sees as he experiences it. As he puts it, what he experiences in nature are "very strong sensations." Because the light and his feelings change so frequently, he is able to paint the same tree, the same mountain, the same rock,

Cézanne going to paint "before his model," as he would say.

over and over again, without them ever seeming the same. He does not seek to imitate nature, but to decipher it, to release its spirit. Like a musician before a score, he interprets. Everything is in the nuances. All is emotion.

Cézanne often paints the sea from L'Estaque.

Quatre-vingt-quinze

'95

In order to do this portrait, Cézanne makes Ambroise Vollard pose for him 115 times. In the end, he declares that he is satisfied only with the "shirt-front."

In 1895, a young art dealer named Ambroise Vollard organizes the first exhibition of Cézanne's works in Paris. A painting of bathers exhibited in the gallery window elicits a strong response. The critics attack what they call his

The invitation announcing Cézanne's exhibition at Vollard's gallery.

"nightmarish vision of atrocities in oil." Cézanne's work is spoken of as a "practical joke." Vollard sells several canvases to collectors, but the most important thing is that the exhibition allows several young painters to discover the work of the Master of Aix. For many, his work is a revelation. At 56, Cézanne finally becomes well-known. Henri Matisse, who is still a young, unknown painter, nearly goes into debt to purchase one of Cézanne's paintings of bathers.

Three Bathers, the painting purchased by Matisse.

Rupture
Break

In 1886, Cézanne breaks with his old friend, Zola. Zola has become rich and famous. His books are awaited as events. His celebrity does not keep him, however, from being one of the first to write articles in defense of the Impressionist painters. He salutes the talents of Manet, Monet, Pissarro and, of course, Cézanne, given that they are friends. But then, little by little, he abandons the cause. In 1877, disillusioned, Zola writes: "the man of genius has not yet arisen." This realization does not change his

Self-portrait against a rose background.

feelings for Paul, however. Zola continues to invite Cézanne to visit and lends him money to help him provide for Hortense and little Paul. Yet the fact remains that Zola does not understand painting. If Paul suffers from this incomprehension, he does not mention it. Nor does he say anything in 1866 when he receives *L'Oeuvre*, Zola's last novel. Although Cézanne remains silent, he cannot keep from recognizing himself in the novel's principle character, a failed, tormented, timid and solitary painter. He thanks Zola for the book, but he knows that their friendship is over. As it turns out, they never see each other again.

Photograph of Zola in his workroom.

Sainte-

A Mountain in Aix

A strange mountain, simultaneously compact and jutting out, which seems both near and far. It overhangs Aix with its undeniable mass, like a bizarre iceberg stranded in the middle of the country. It is hard not to see it. It rises above the wall of the Jas de Bouffan, it appears in the bend of the smallest footpath. For Cézanne, Mount Sainte-Victoire is like magic. He paints under its spell. As others paint the face of their beloved over and over again, Cézanne

Mount Sainte-Victoire as seen from the Bibémus quarry.

Victoire

paints his mountain from all angles, in all kinds of weather. He never abandons it. Throughout his life, he continues to recreate that commanding presence of his childhood. In a number of paintings, the mountain almost consumes the entire canvas, becoming an enormous triangle looming against the horizon. The colors blend so that the sky is infused

To convey "the feel" of the air, Cézanne blends his colors into a blue-tinted light.

with green and the mountain with blue. In his blending of colors, something remarkable happens: the mountain seems to evaporate, fusing with the airiness of the sky.

Touches

Daubs

Cézanne works with touches: with little daubs of color placed side by side, and with large vigorous strokes superimposed upon each other. In explaining his use of this technique, Cézanne says: "I am unable to convey my sensation immediately; therefore, I put the color down again and again, however I can." However he can? Perhaps, but never without full attention to what he is doing. The testaments of those who knew him make it clear that Cézanne never did anything without having fully thought it through. Cézanne does what he means to do. His progression through touches of paint is particularly visible in a number of his watercolors. Playing upon the transparency of colors, their layering, and their contrast with the white of the paper, Cézanne creates mosaics as light as air.

By the end of his life, Cézanne had painted more than 650 watercolors.

Cézanne abandons the thick
paste of his early years. His
materials are now more fluid.

hUé

Jeered

In Aix, there are many who mock the solitary Cézanne, who has the wild hair of a bandit and paints so strangely. At times, gangs of children follow behind him throwing stones. He is considered an eccentric, a "fada" as one says in the South of France. Cézanne suffers from not being recognized as an important painter. He encloses himself in the world of his painting. As he gets older, the lively, highly sensitive Cézanne prefers the apples and the

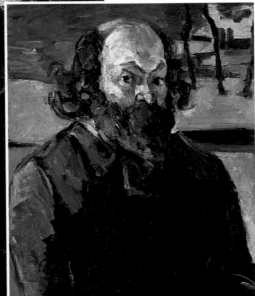

Self-portrait.

Vallier, the gardener.

landscapes of Provence to his compatriots, who are no better than a bunch of "idiots, cretins and fools." When he is swept up by the desire to paint a portrait, he derives more pleasure from painting Vallier, his old gardener, than the notables of Aix. He fears "busybodies" who think only of getting him into their "clutches." In fact, he is never as well as when he is alone with his work. For this reason, he rarely lives with "the Ball," which is what he calls his wife. He feels quite differently about his son, however, for whom he has a genuine attachment, and who, as a child, is allowed to play the game of opening the actual doors and windows of the houses which serve as his father's subject.

Va-et-vient

Vacillation

Cézanne is unpredictable. He is at the mercy of his moods: everything changes depending on whether he feels enthusiastic or discouraged. If a painting is going well, he is full of faith. If, on the other hand, it goes poorly, he is overwhelmed by doubt. His life is dominated by his work. There is an unusual violence in Cézanne, a violence which he subdues through painting. If, however, he does not obtain the result which he desires, then there is nothing to keep him from flying into a rage. Frequently,

Thanks to his inheritance from his father, Cézanne is free to paint for himself, without having to worry about earning his living.

Even though she rarely lives with Cézanne, Hortense is one of the few who has the patience to pose regularly for him.

when a canvas has failed to satisfy him, he will destroy it or throw it out of the window into the garden. However, Cézanne also knows how to be patient. He devotes an infinite amount of time to working on his paintings, sometimes months and even years. At times, he takes a week simply to set the scene of a still-life and to choose his colors. To finish a still-life, he may need more than one hundred sessions, and to complete a portrait, even more than that. It is not time which concerns Cézanne, however. It is the result which counts. His habit is to retouch a canvas as many times as he thinks necessary. Another form of vacillation.

Wagner

A musician himself—as a youth he plays the clarinet—Cézanne is around twenty when he discovers the music of Wagner. He is greatly excited by the power of Wagner's opera, *Tannhäuser.* For him, the music rises like a wild wave. This, of course, is not everyone's opinion. When the opera is performed for the first time, it is booed. People even come to blows over it. Faced with a scandal of great magnitude, Wagner withdraws his score. Cézanne, however, feels close to this composer, whose music heralds a new age. Years later, this is

"Cézanne's studies are like the echoes of a melody," writes the poet, Rainer Maria Rilke.

Richard Wagner

Cézanne entitles this painting, *Overture to Tannhäuser*.

precisely what Cézanne will do in painting, through envisioning the relationship between colors and forms in space in a new way.

aiX

Cézanne's last studio, on the hill of Lauves.

Aix, always Aix. For Cézanne, all pathways lead to Aix. Not once in his life does he cross either seas or frontiers. His territory is his village in the heart of Provence. His world is made up of Aix and its surroundings: the village of Tholonet, the steep banks of the Arc river, Bibémus quarry, and the Château Noir. He speaks with deep tenderness of Aix's arid gorges, rocky footpaths, and long-needled pines bent by Mistral* winds. He knows the Aix countryside to its depths: each rock, each shrub, each

Geraniums in the garden.

corner of the moor.
No sooner has he
left Aix, than he
misses it. About this
he says, "When
you're born there,
you're done for,
nothing else speaks
to you."

* Northern winds in the
South of France

Even though most painters live near
Paris, Cézanne ultimately retreats to
Provence. He is the Master of Aix.

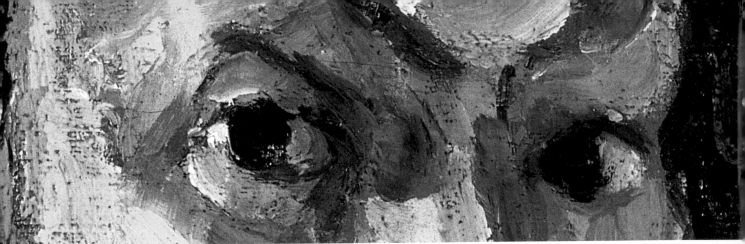

Yeux

Eyes

Cézanne rarely paints from memory. He has the need to see. It is with his eyes that he captures his "colored sensations." He leaves the house with his easel, paints, paper or canvas to paint Mount Sainte-Victoire or the rocks of Bibémus. It is essential for him to breathe the air of the moor, to feel the wind on his face, to measure the strength of the sun. His enthusiasm takes him so far that he almost burns his eyes. On October 15, 1906, a storm overtakes him while he is painting. He falls ill and loses

consciousness. He dies
eight days later. His death
comes almost as he would
have willed it. As he swore
to himself a month earlier,
"to die while painting
rather than foundering in
over-ripeness.…"

oseZ

Let Us Dare

To a critic who mocks his work, Cézanne retorts: "Me, I dare...I dare. I have the courage of my opinions. He laughs best who laughs last." While Cézanne speaks boldly of daring, he also remains humble and uncertain. Several weeks before his death, in September 1906, he says: "It seems to me that my progress is slow." Until the end, Cézanne will have thought that he lacked the ability to accomplish his task. "I glimpse the Promised Land, but will I be able to penetrate through to it?" Not only does he reach it, but he carries generations of painters in his train. After Cézanne, painting is no longer what it was before him. Cézanne shows the way of an extraordinary freedom. "Let us dare," says his work. His message has been heard. Others have dared, many others after him.

"I am the primitive of a new art," said Cézanne.

Acknowledgments

Cover: *Child in a Straw Hat,* c. 1896, painting (detail), ©
1995, Los Angeles County Museum of Art, Los Angeles.
Apples and Biscuits (detail), see page 26.

Endpapers: *Mount Sainte-Victoire as seen from Bibémus
Quarry,* c. 1898, painting (details), The Baltimore Museum
of Art, Baltimore.

Pages 6–7: Louis–Auguste Cézanne, photograph,
Documentation Center, Musée d'Orsay, Paris. Detail of an
illustrated letter from Cézanne to Zola, ink, c. October 19,
1866, collection Le Blond-Zola. *The Great Pine,* c. 1890,
watercolor (detail), © 1995, Kunsthaus, Zurich.

Pages 8–9: *Bather with Arms at His Sides,* c. 1885, painting
(detail), private collection. *The Bather,* c. 1859, ink (detail),
private collection. *Woman Diving into the Water,* c.
1867–70, water color and gouache, National Museum of
Wales, Cardiff.

Pages 10–11: *The Painter,* c. 1868–71, drawing, Öffentliche
Kunstsammlung, Bâle. *Portrait of the Artist's Father,* c.
1866, painting (detail), National Gallery of Art,
Washington.

Pages 12–13: *The Four Seasons,* c. 1860–62, paintings, Musée
du Petit Palais, Paris. Photographs from the photo archives
of the Musées de la Ville de Paris, © by SPADEM.

Pages 14–15: *Self-Portrait,* c. 1861, private collection.
Photograph of Émile Zola, c. 1865, collection Dr. F. Émile
Zola. *Paris: Quai de Bercy-Wine Market,* c. 1872, private
collection, Geneva.

Pages 16–17: *Venus* (after Raphael), c. 1866–69, drawing,
private collection. *Scipio,* c. 1867, painting, Museu de Arte
de Sao Paulo Assis Chateaubriand, Sau Paulo. Photo by
Luiz Hossaka.

Pages 18–19: *The Lawyer,* c. 1866, painting (detail), Musée
d'Orsay, Paris. Photo from the Réunion des Musées
Nationaux (R.M.N.). *Portrait of Achille Emperaire,* c.
1868–70, painting, Musée d'Orsay, Paris. Photo R.M.N.
Head of Achille Emperaire, c. 1867–70, drawing,
Department of Graphic Arts, Musée du Louvre, Paris.
Property of the Musée d'Orsay. Photo R.M.N.

Pages 20–21: *Madame Cézanne in a Red Armchair,* 1877–78,
painting, Museum of Fine Arts, Boston. *Houses of
L'Estaque,* c. 1882–85, painting, National Gallery of Art,
Washington. *Studies and Portraits of the Artist's Son,*
drawing (detail), Graphische Sammlung Albertina, Vienna.

Pages 22–23: *Portrait of Camille Pissarro,* c. 1873, drawing,
Department of Graphic Arts, Musée du Louvre, Paris.
Property of the Musée d'Orsay. Photo R.M.N. Cézanne and
Pissarro in the company of two other painters in the Auvers
region, c. 1873, photograph, Documentation Center, Musée
d'Orsay, Paris. *The Bridge at Maincy,* c. 1879, painting,
Musée d'Orsay, Paris. Photo R.M.N.

Pages 24–25: *Pool at the Jas de Bouffan,* c. 1878, collection
Corinne Cuellar, Zurich. The Jas de Bouffan, photograph,
private collection. *The Card Players,* c. 1890–92, painting,
Musée d'Orsay, Paris. Photo R.M.N.

Pages 26–27: *Apples and Biscuits,* c. 1879–82, painting,
Musée de l'Orangerie, Paris. Photo R.M.N. *Still Life,* c.

1890–94, painting, © 1995, Kunsthaus, Zurich.
Pages 28–29: *Mill on a River,* c. 1904–05, watercolor, Elke Walford Fotowerkstatt, Hamburger Kunsthalle, Hamburg. *Houses in Provence,* c. 1879–82, painting, National Gallery of Art, Washington.
Pages 30–31: *Still Life with a Plaster Cupid,* c. 1892–95, painting, The Courtauld Institute Galleries, London. Photo Gordon H. Roberton, A.C. Cooper Ltd. *Plaster Cupid,* c. 1900–04, watercolor, The Pierpont Morgan Library, New York, private collection. *Green Pitcher,* c. 1885–87, watercolor, Department of Graphic Arts, Musée du Louvre, Paris. Photo R.M.N. *Still Life with Fruit Basket,* c. 1888–90, painting, Musée d'Orsay, Paris. Photo R.M.N.
Pages 32–33: *Bathers,* c. 1874–75, painting, The Metropolitan Museum, New York. Cézanne before his *Great Bathers,* photograph by Émile Bernard, c. 1904, Archives Vollard, Musée d'Orsay, Paris.
Pages 34–35: *Bibémus,* c. 1895, painting, Museum Folkwang, Essen. *Great Bathers,* c. 1906, painting (detail), Philadelphia Museum, Philadelphia.
Pages 36–37: Photograph of Cézanne on his way to work in Auvers, c. 1873, Department of Graphic Arts, Musée du Louvre, Paris. Property of Musée d'Orsay. *The Sea from L'Estaque,* c. 1878–79, painting, Musée Picasso. Photo R.M.N.
Pages 38–39: *Portrait of Ambroise Vollard,* c. 1899, painting, Musée du Petit Palais. Photo from the photo archives of the Musées de la Ville de Paris, © by SPADEM.
Pages 40–41: *Self-Portrait against a Rose Background,* c. 1875, painting, private collection. Photo by Martine Beck Coppola. Émile Zola in his study at Medan, photograph by Dornac Paris, Archives Larousse-Giraudon.

Pages 42–43: *Mount Sainte-Victoire seen from Bibémus,* c. 1897, The Baltimore Museum of Art, Baltimore. *Mount Sainte-Victoire,* c. 1885–87, The Courtauld Institute Galleries, London. Photo by Gordon H. Roberton, A.C. Cooper Ltd.
Pages 44–45: *Trees and Rocks at the Château Noir,* c. 1895–98, Musée Granet, Aix–en–Provence. Photo by Bernard Terlay. *Mount Sainte–Victoire,* c. 1902, painting. Gallery Beyeler, Bâle.
Pages 46–47: *Self–Portrait,* c. 1873–76, Musée d'Orsay, Paris. Photo R.M.N. *Portrait of Vallier,* c. 1906, watercolor, The National Gallery, London.
Pages 48–49: *Self Portrait with Palette,* c. 1890, painting, Foundation E.G. Bührle, Zurich. Photo by Drayer. *Madame Cézanne in a Striped Dress,* c. 1883–85, painting, Philadelphia Museum of Art, Philadelphia.
Pages 50–51: Richard Wagner, engraving, photo by Lauros-Giradon. *Overture to Tannhäuser,* c. 1868–69, painting, The Hermitage Museum, St. Petersburg. Overture to Tannhäuser, score by Richard Wagner (rights reserved).
Pages 52–53: Cézanne's studio at Les Lauves, photograph, © Sabine Rewald. *Pots of Flowers,* c. 1885, painting, Musée du Louvre, Paris. Property of the Musée d'Orsay. Photo R.M.N. *Chestnut-Trees at the Jas de Bouffan in Winter,* c. 1885–86, painting, The Minneapolis Institute of Arts, Minneapolis.
Pages 54–55: *Self-Portrait* (detail), see page 46. Cézanne working outdoors, photograph, c. 1906, © A. Salomon.
Pages 56–57: *The Garden at Les Lauves,* c. 1906, painting, The Phillips Collection, Washington.